The first true dinosaurs evolved 230 million years ago, and for the next 165 million years they dominated life on the land. They ranged in size from animals no bigger than a chicken to giants ten times bigger than an elephant. There were dinosaurs in practically every part of the world.

In this book we  fascinating animals and at the world in which they lived. Beginning with the early dinosaurs of the Triassic Period, from 250 to 210 million years ago, we move on to the Jurassic Period, between 210 and 145 million years ago, when great numbers of new forms of dinosaur evolved, and finish with the Cretaceous Period, from 145 to 65 million years ago, when the dinosaurs reached their peak of development before meeting an as yet unexplained end.

LIFE ON THE SUPERCONTINENT

Imagine you are in a spacecraft orbiting the Earth 230 million years ago in the middle of the Triassic Period. The planet turning below you looks very different from the one we know today. The familiar continents – North and South America, Africa, Asia, Europe – are not there. Instead there is just a single massive landmass, the supercontinent of Pangaea, surrounded by the world-spanning Tethys Sea.

Most of Pangaea lay outside the polar regions and the climate during this time was warmer than it is now. There were no ice caps – even at the poles the temperature ranged between 10 and 20°C. In the centre of Pangaea, far from the ocean, conditions were hot and dry and deserts formed.

Plants adapted to dry conditions, such as tree ferns, conifers and cycads, a type of plant rather like a palm tree, grew in vast forests. No flowers bloomed in this landscape – flowering plants would not evolve for another 80 million years or so.

The coming of the dinosaurs
Reptiles were the dominant four-legged land animals. Among them were a group called the thecodonts. Most thecodonts were meat eaters, but a few became plant eaters. One

Over 230 million years ago all of the world's land was gathered together in the supercontinent of Pangaea.

type of thecodont took up life along riverbanks. Its descendants became the crocodiles, and are still there today.

Towards the end of the Triassic Period a new type of four-legged animal began to appear on Earth. Thecodonts and other reptiles disappeared to be replaced by one of the most successful groups of animals of all time. These were also descendants of the thecodonts – the dinosaurs.

There were two-legged, meat-eating dinosaurs, and small two-legged and giant four-legged plant-eaters. With few barriers to the movement of life across the surface of the land the dinosaurs began to spread out across the world.

PLATEOSAURUS

The land that would one day be Europe was a very different place in Triassic times. It was hot and dry, much nearer the Equator than it is now. One of the animals that lived here was *Plateosaurus*, one of a group of dinosaurs called the prosauropods. *Plateosaurus* mostly ate plants, although it may also have swallowed the odd small animal whenever it got the chance!

Plateosaurus was a big animal for its time, measuring 8 metres (26 feet) from tailtip to nose. It walked on all fours, but when it wanted to reach some succulent leaves high up on a tree it could rear up on its back legs, using its massive tail for extra support.

Herds of *Plateosaurus* roamed the hot plains of Triassic Europe and probably further afield too. We know they travelled together in large herds because the fossil remains of dozens of these animals were found in one spot near the town of Trossingen in Germany. It is possible that this particular herd all died together when a flash-flood swept across a dried up river bed as the herd crossed it.

Plateosaurus *could rear up on its hind legs to bring high up leaves within reach. Its tail gave extra support as it ate.*

Plateosaurus

Plateosaurus

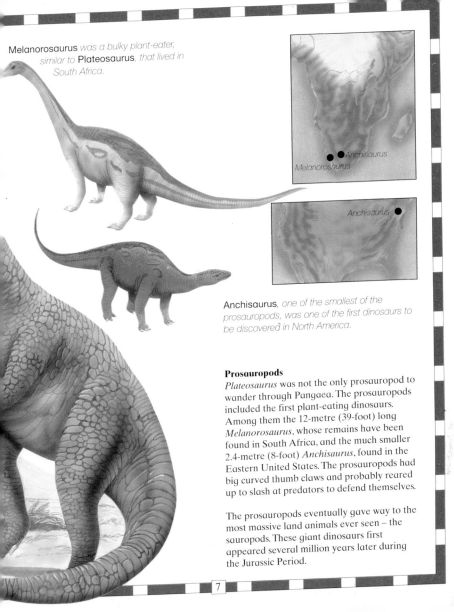

Melanorosaurus *was a bulky plant-eater,*
similar to **Plateosaurus***, that lived in*
South Africa.

●● *Anchisaurus*
Melanorosaurus

Anchisaurus ●

Anchisaurus, *one of the smallest of the*
prosauropods, was one of the first dinosaurs to
be discovered in North America.

Prosauropods

Plateosaurus was not the only prosauropod to
wander through Pangaea. The prosauropods
included the first plant-eating dinosaurs.
Among them the 12-metre (39-foot) long
Melanorosaurus, whose remains have been
found in South Africa, and the much smaller
2.4-metre (8-foot) *Anchisaurus*, found in the
Eastern United States. The prosauropods had
big curved thumb claws and probably reared
up to slash at predators to defend themselves.

The prosauropods eventually gave way to the
most massive land animals ever seen – the
sauropods. These giant dinosaurs first
appeared several million years later during
the Jurassic Period.

HERRERASAURUS

Herrerasaurus was one of the first dinosaurs to appear on Earth, perhaps as long as 230 million years ago. It was also one of the first theropods, the meat-eating dinosaurs. It was a 3-metre (10-foot) long predator, which hunted reptiles in upland regions of what is now South America. At this time 'South America' was further south than today and firmly attached to Africa!

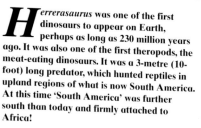

The country that *Herrerasaurus* inhabited would have had a long dry season followed by a rainy season that brought forth lush plant growth. No doubt *Herrerasaurus* would have made use of the plant cover to wait in ambush for a likely meal. It was also able to run at speed on its powerful hind legs and would have been capable of launching darting attacks on larger animals. Its sharp claws and teeth would have been used to weaken and disable its prey before killing it.

Triassic theropods

The theropods were the meat-eating dinosaurs. Some of them may have been fast-moving warm-blooded animals. Among this group were some of the fiercest and most awesome predators of all time, as well as tiny killers no bigger than today's songbirds.

Herrerasaurus were fast-moving hunters and soon replaced other reptile predators of the Triassic world.

The Triassic theropods included *Staurikosaurus*, which was similar to *Herrerasaurus* but slightly smaller. It lived in Brazil. *Coelophysis* hunted in packs across land that now forms part of the Western USA. These 3-metre (10-foot) long hunters must have been a fearsome sight when they attacked together. Their strength in numbers would also make it difficult for other animals to attack them.

Staurikosaurus, *though smaller than* **Herrerasaurus**, *was still a deadly hunter.*

The remains of huge herds of **Coelophysis** *have been discovered. Hundreds of these animals may have fed together.*

LESOTHOSAURUS

*L*esothosaurus was a desert dinosaur that lived around 190 million years ago, right at the end of the Triassic period. Its remains have been found in the northern part of South America, in Venezuela, and in South Africa, proving that these two continents must once have been joined. After all, it isn't very likely that a 1-metre (3-foot) dinosaur could swim the Atlantic Ocean!

These little dinosaurs browsed through the desert plants in herds. They had no weapons, such as thumb claws or armoured skin, with which to defend themselves against predators. Instead they had to be alert for any signs of danger and ready to run for safety at high speed. *Lesothosaurus's* long back legs give us a clue that it was something of a sprinter.

Some people believe that *Lesothosaurus* escaped from the heat and drought of the summer by lying dormant in burrows until the rains came again and there was food to eat. Some present-day crocodiles will also do this.

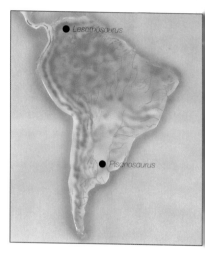

A **Lesothosaurus** *at full speed would have been very difficult to catch.*

Ornithischians

Lesothosaurus belonged to a group of dinosaurs called the ornithischians, which first appeared towards the end of the Triassic. Ornithischians had hip-bones that were arranged rather like those of a modern-day bird. One of the first of these dinosaurs was *Pisanosaurus*, which was slightly smaller than *Lesothosaurus*. Its remains have been found in Argentina.

Lesothosaurus may have been one of the first of a branch of the ornithischians called ornithopods. The feet of these animals were something like a bird's, with the first toe facing backwards. In fact, the name ornithopod means 'bird-foot'. Like *Lesothosaurus* all of the early ornithopods were two-legged plant eaters. There were few Triassic ornithischians but they became more common in the Jurassic and Cretaceous periods that followed.

● *Lesothosaurus*

The small **Pisanosaurus** *was one of the first plant-eating dinosaurs to appear on Earth.*

THE GREAT CRACK UP

Great changes were occurring during the Jurassic Period. Slowly, very slowly, Pangaea was splitting apart. North America began to separate from North Africa and a new ocean – the Central Atlantic – came into being. Red hot lava flowed from immense cracks in the Earth's surface as the continents drifted away from one another. Great mountain chains were thrown up in North America and volcanoes erupted in South America.

The world's climate was still warm, as it had been in the Triassic Period, but now, as new seas formed in Pangaea, moist winds began to blow. Rain swept over lands that had been deserts and plants soon spread to take advantage of the new more favourable conditions. There were still no flowering plants, but tall conifer forests were common, with trees similar to the giant sequoias and pine trees of today. Ferns and horsetails grew abundantly, providing a source of food for the big plant-eating dinosaurs that followed the advance of the plants.

A dinosaur explosion

The dividing of Pangaea had another effect on the dinosaurs. Before, the same types of dinosaurs had been found throughout the world. Now new oceans and mountain chains began to split dinosaur populations apart. Isolated from each other, they began to evolve in different ways and new types of dinosaur appeared.

The Triassic prosauropods gave way to the mighty sauropods, immense plant-eaters that could strip vegetation from the ground to the treetops. Ornithischian dinosaurs took on strange new forms in the shape of the armoured stegosaurs. Hunting them all were the fearsome carnosaurs, including the awesome *Allosaurus*, undisputed heavyweight champion of the Jurassic world. Perhaps most extraordinary of all, one branch of the theropods took a direction that led to a completely new form of animal. They developed feathers and became birds.

The Jurassic Period saw the birth of the Atlantic Ocean as the continents began to drift apart.

DIPLODOCUS

A herd of *Diplodocus* browsing through a Jurassic forest in the Western USA must have been an amazing sight. From end to end *Diplodocus* measured 27 metres (90 feet), much bigger than the earlier prosauropods like *Plateosaurus*. Half of this length was its long tail, carried above the ground like a whip, ready to lash at any predator that had the nerve to approach from behind. An elephant would have looked tiny next to this animal. However, *Diplodocus* was lightly built despite its length. At 12 tons it would have been only two to three times heavier than an elephant.

At 27 metres from nose to tail tip Diplodocus *was one of the longest animals ever to walk on land.*

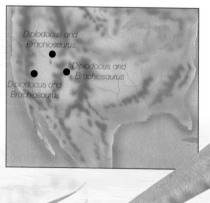

Diplodocus and Brachiosaurus

Diplodocus and Brachiosaurus

Diplodocus and Brachiosaurus

Everything, from the ferns of the forest floor to the upper branches of the conifers and gingkoes came within reach of the long-necked *Diplodocus*. Some people believe that it could extend its reach upwards by rising up on its back legs, using its tail for extra support. Once they had stripped bare the plant cover from one area the herd moved on together to new feeding grounds.

14

The 30 to 50 ton **Brachiosaurus** *was one of the biggest and heaviest of all the dinosaurs.*

throughout the world by the late Jurassic.

Brachiosaurus was shorter than *Diplodocus* at a mere 25 metres (80 feet) or so, but it may have weighed as much as 50 tons! *Brachiosaurus* remains have been found near those of *Diplodocus* in the Western USA, as well as in Europe and Africa.

The first sauropod to be discovered was *Cetiosaurus*. Fossil bones of this animal were unearthed at various locations in England in the early nineteenth century. These were among the first clues that life on Earth had changed over vast periods of time.

Jurassic sauropods

Big though it certainly was, *Diplodocus* was not the biggest of the sauropods. This group of dinosaurs evolved from the earlier prosauropods of Triassic and early Jurassic times. By the middle of the Jurassic the prosauropods had disappeared altogether. Herds of massive sauropods were common

STEGOSAURUS

One of the most unusual Jurassic sights would have been a big *Stegosaurus* snuffling along as it browsed over the wooded plains of North America snipping off choice pieces of plant with its beak-like snout.

This 9-metre (30-foot) ornithischian had a double row of big bony plates running the length of its back. Some of the plates were as much as 75 centimetres (2.5 feet) high, but although impressive they were probably not strong enough to protect the *Stegosaurus* from attack. Some people now believe that the plates were well supplied with blood vessels and were used to control the animal's body temperature. Whenever it wanted to warm up it would stand side on to the sun, collecting warmth through its plates. The plates would also act like radiators when the *Stegosaurus* moved into the shade, helping the animal to lose heat if it got too hot.

At the end of the *Stegosaurus's* tail there were four massive spikes. These were its defence against big predators like *Allosaurus*. It could swing its tail from side to side like a great club. *Stegosaurus* may hold one rather odd dinosaur record. It is possible that it had the smallest brain for its size of any dinosaur. However, since there were *Stegosaurus* around for 10 million years maybe it wasn't that stupid!

Stegosaurus
Stegosaurus *Stegosaurus*

Stegosaurus's *back plates may have been brightly coloured and used for display.*

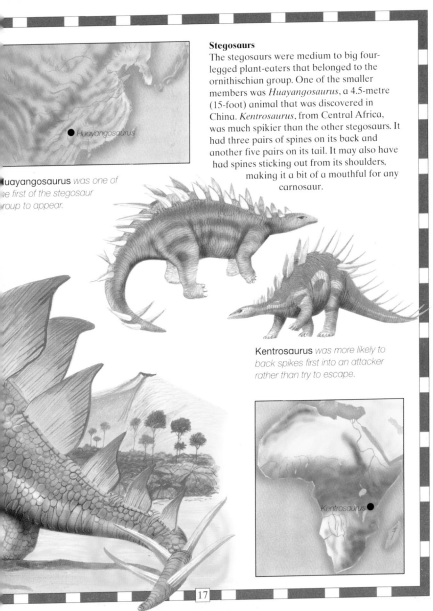

Stegosaurs

The stegosaurs were medium to big four-legged plant-eaters that belonged to the ornithischian group. One of the smaller members was *Huayangosaurus*, a 4.5-metre (15-foot) animal that was discovered in China. *Kentrosaurus*, from Central Africa, was much spikier than the other stegosaurs. It had three pairs of spines on its back and another five pairs on its tail. It may also have had spines sticking out from its shoulders, making it a bit of a mouthful for any carnosaur.

Huayangosaurus was one of the first of the stegosaur group to appear.

Kentrosaurus *was more likely to back spikes first into an attacker rather than try to escape.*

ALLOSAURUS

There probably weren't many Jurassic animals that could have stood up to *Allosaurus*. It was 11 metres (36 feet) long and about 2 tons of muscle and razor sharp teeth. *Allosaurus* has been found all over North America, as well as in Africa and Australia. There must have been few places where plant eaters could browse in safety without fear of an *Allosaurus* attack. To make things worse, it seems likely that bands of *Allosaurus* roamed together looking for herds of sauropods to attack.

Compsognath

Allosaurus

An attacking two-ton **Allosaurus** *was a fearsome sight.*

In contrast to mighty **Allosaurus**, **Compsognathus** *was a tiny killer, not much bigger than a cat.*

Archaeopteryx *may have made gliding flights from branch to branch after climbing up trees with its claws.*

Allosaurus was fearsomely equipped for its role as a predator. Its jaws didn't just open up, they also expanded sideways so that it could take a huge bite from its victim. Its arms were fairly short, and couldn't be used for walking, but they were tipped with powerful claws that could be used to hold on to the prey while the powerful jaws did their deadly work.

Jurassic theropods

The Jurassic hunters were not all big killers like *Allosaurus*. *Compsognathus* was a slim, lightly-built animal about 1 metre (3 feet) long, but to the lizards and other small animals it hunted it was a deadly predator. *Compsognathus* has been found in France and Germany. These places are in the heart of Europe now, but when *Compsognathus* lived they were semi-desert islands.

The Archaeopterygidae are a particularly interesting theropod family. One of them, *Archaeopteryx*, is one of the most famous fossil finds of all. It lived on the same European desert islands as *Compsognathus* and was similar in size and build to that dinosaur. However, *Archaeopteryx* had one important feature that set it apart – it had feathers, making it the oldest bird ever found. Today's birds are the living descendants of the dinosaurs.

A WORLD APART

By the start of the Cretaceous Period Pangaea had really begun to break up. The Central Atlantic was becoming ever wider and the South Atlantic began to open up as Africa separated from South America. Great inland areas of the continents were flooded by new seas. North America and Europe were still linked but West and East North America were split in two by the Mid-Continental Seaway and the Turgai Sea separated Europe from Asia.

Over the course of the Cretaceous Period the gaps between the continents widened as the oceans opened up and shallow seas flooded much of the land.

Overall the Earth was warm and dry, but different regions had distinct climates depending on how far from the Equator they were. On the shores of the shrinking Tethys Sea the climate was still tropical and subtropical. Further north and south there were cooler forested lands, though these were still warmer and wetter than today.

To begin with the plants that grew in the Cretaceous were very similar to those that grew in the Jurassic period. Conifers, gingkoes and ferns were still common.

However, at some point in the Cretaceous there was a major development in the plants. Somewhere, possibly in a valley between West Africa and South America, the first flowering plants appeared. These first flowers may have been similar to today's magnolias but all we have to go on are some pollen grains. By the end of the Cretaceous Period flowering plants had spread throughout the world.

As the world divided into separate landmasses so the dinosaurs continued to develop in different ways. In the northern continents in particular, several new types of dinosaur appeared. The stegosaurs were replaced by the armoured ankylosaurs, low-slung plant-eaters that often had tails with heavy bony clubs. Duck-billed hadrosaurs, a type of ornithopod equipped to feed on tough vegetation, were found in the marshes around the inland seas. Ceratopsians, the horn-faced dinosaurs, such as *Triceratops*, roamed around in herds through the forests of North America. The meat-eating dinosaurs ranged from the ostrich-sized coelurosaurs to the powerful *Tyrannosaurus*, a fearsome killing machine that might have made even *Allosaurus* pause.

MINMI

Minmi is one of the few dinosaurs to have been found in Australia. This isn't because there were fewer dinosaurs in Australia than elsewhere. It is just that it is not easy to find fossils in the rocks there and organised searches have only been carried out over the last 15 years or so.

Minmi was 3 metres (10 feet) long and was one of the most heavily armoured of all animals. It used to be thought of as a type of ankylosaur but it might be the only member yet found of a completely new family of armoured dinosaur. Bony armour covered almost all of *Minmi's* body, from its tough box-shaped skull to the triangular plates that protected its tail. Even its belly was covered in bony plates. Any predator that tried to take a bite from *Minmi* risked breaking some teeth.

Ankylosaurs

If *Minmi* wasn't actually an ankylosaur it was at least closely related to those animals. Ankylosaurs had first appeared during the Jurassic Period but it was in the Cretaceous Period that they really became successful. They were sturdy animals with bony armour and often had spikes protecting their backs. Some, such as *Euoplocephalus*, one of the most common ankylosaurs of North America, had a huge bone club at the end of its muscular tail. One blow from this would no doubt discourage most predators. The 7-metre (23-foot), 4-ton *Edmontonia* was a formidable opponent that used its body armour for attack as well as defence. It had long spines on its shoulders that could do great damage to the legs of an attacking carnosaur.

An ankylosaur is also one of the very few dinosaurs to have been found in Antarctica. But when you consider the difficulties of finding fossils under a great thickness of ice it isn't really surprising that so few have been found there.

Minmi's *body armour kept it safe from most attacks.*

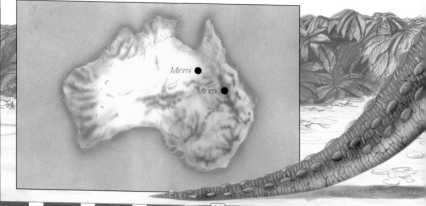

Edmontonia *(top left)* and **Euoplocephalus** *(bottom left)* protected themselves with spines and club tails. An ankylosaur *(below)* is the only dinosaur to have been found so far in Antarctica.

23

TRICERATOPS

Nine metres (30 feet) long and weighing over 5 tons apiece, a herd of *Triceratops* were like a tank battalion on the move as they wandered through the open woodlands of North America at the end of the Cretaceous Period. A *Triceratops's* head alone was as long as the average human body. A great bony frill stuck out from the back of the skull, protecting the animal's neck. Two massive horns of bone jutted out above its eyes with a third, smaller horn on its nose. The rhinoceros of today has horns made of highly compacted hair. *Triceratops's* horns were of bone and grew directly from its skull.

Triceratops were plant-eaters and it is most likely that *Triceratops* males used their horns to battle other males for control of a herd. Scarred neck frills and cheek bones that have been found suggest wounds suffered in such contests. There is no doubt, however, that a herd of *Triceratops* would have presented a formidable challenge to any predator.

Triceratops was probably among the last of the dinosaurs to appear on Earth, and one of the last to become extinct.

Ceratopsids

The ceratopsids or horn-faced dinosaurs were all plant-eating ornithischians. They were common in North America during the Late Cretaceous Period. *Centrosaurus* was smaller than *Triceratops* and had one long nose horn and two much smaller eyebrow horns. Huge herds of *Centrosaurus* lived in the forests of what is now part of Canada. *Styracosaurus* was smaller still, a mere 5.5 metres (18 feet) long, but it had a spectacular neck frill with six long spikes, four of which were longer than a person's arm. *Styracosaurus* also had a large nose horn. This formidable armament must

have given the animals some protection against the big predators such as *Tyrannosaurus*.

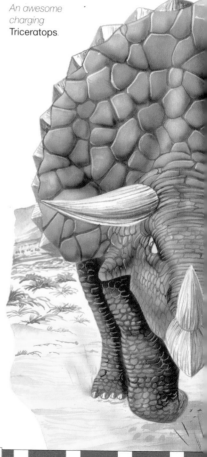

An awesome charging Triceratops.

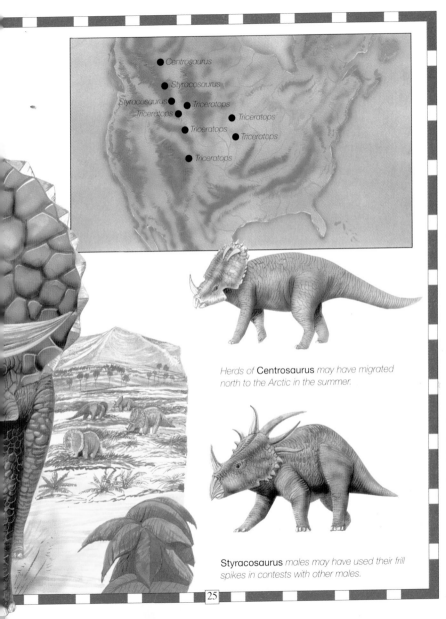

Herds of **Centrosaurus** may have migrated north to the Arctic in the summer.

Styracosaurus males may have used their frill spikes in contests with other males.

25

TYRANNOSAURUS

Tyrannosaurus was possibly the most powerful predator that has ever walked on land. It was only a metre or so longer than *Allosaurus* but it weighed three times as much. *Tyrannosaurus*'s great head was just over a metre (4 feet) long and it was armed with teeth that were 18 centimetres (7 inches) in length with serrated edges like a bread knife. Teeth like this would have cut through the toughest dinosaur hide with ease when the huge jaws closed on *Tyrannosaurus*'s victim.

Tyrannosaurus remains have been found throughout western North America from New Mexico to Canada. Even the largest plant-eater living in this region wouldn't have been safe from a *Tyrannosaurus* attack. It is possible that these mighty killers may have attacked in packs, making a successful kill even more certain.

One of the oddest things about *Tyrannosaurus* were its tiny arms. They were so short that they couldn't even be used to take food to the animal's mouth. However, each arm was powerful enough to lift two grown men and it

is possible that they were used to lift *Tyrannosaurus* up from a resting position on the ground. Like *Allosaurus*, *Tyrannosaurus* may also have used its sharp claws to hold on to its prey while the deadly jaws descended.

*The awesome **Tyrannosaurus** was possibly the biggest, most powerful hunter that has ever lived on land.*

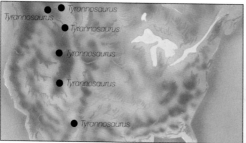

Tyrannosaurus
Tyrannosaurus
Tyrannosaurus
Tyrannosaurus
Tyrannosaurus
Tyrannosaurus

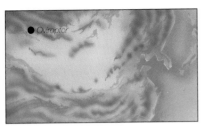

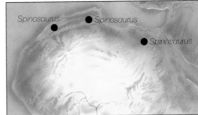

Oviraptor *didn't have much defence if it was caught stealing a big dinosaur's eggs and risked being stamped to death.*

Some people believe that **Spinosaurus** *may have lived on a diet of fish rather than eating other dinosaurs.*

Cretaceous theropods

Tyrannosaurus, though undoubtedly the biggest killer around in the Cretaceous Period, was by no means the only one. One of the more unusual was *Spinosaurus*, a dinosaur found in North Africa. On its back there was a skin sail held up by props of bone like the ribs in an umbrella. It is not certain what the sail was used for but it may have acted as a heat collector, helping the animal to warm up in the morning. *Oviraptor* was a meat-eater without teeth that lived on a diet of eggs. This 2-metre (6.5-foot) dinosaur lived in Mongolia where it raided the nests of other dinosaurs, stealing their eggs and puncturing them with two bony prongs that stuck out from the roof of its mouth.

WHERE DID THEY GO?

From their first appearance 230 million years ago to the puzzle of their disappearance 166 million years later dinosaurs dominated life on the land. What happened to wipe out such a successful group? There are a lot of ideas, but there are no answers.

The catastrophe that struck the dinosaurs also wiped out many other forms of life. The flying pterosaurs disappeared from the skies, and the plesiosaurs and ichthyosaurs vanished from the oceans. All four-legged land animals heavier than about 10 kilograms (22 pounds) became extinct.

One of the more spectacular ideas put forward suggests that a large asteroid collided with the Earth. The titanic explosion that resulted sent up huge clouds of gas and dust that were swept around the Earth's upper atmosphere, blocking out the heat and light from the sun. The changes that resulted in the Earth's climate may have been enough to kill off the dinosaurs and other animals that vanished.